AF255642

FATHER

FATHER

A Collection of Poems

ABHILASH FRAIZER

RESOURCE *Publications* · Eugene, Oregon

FATHER
A Collection of Poems

Resource Publications
An Imprint of Wipf and Stock Publishers
199 W. 8th Ave., Suite 3
Eugene, OR 97401

www.wipfandstock.com

PAPERBACK ISBN: 978-1-6667-8781-8
HARDCOVER ISBN: 978-1-6667-8782-5
EBOOK ISBN: 978-1-6667-8783-2

Dedicated
To My Wife
SUNITHA

Table of Contents

SUN IN THE RAIN

How does it feel
Sitting lonely in the rain?
How does it feel
To bereave the Beloved,
– God and Master –
And sit lonely in the rain?

The rain that began
At the hour of His dreadful death,
Has not yet stopped;
It keeps weeping all through the night,
Just as my bereaved soul.

Do you know how it feels
To lose God?
A feeling from time immemorial,
Starting from the days of Adam
In the Paradise that was lost!

Alas!
Paradise keeps losing
Time and again in history.
And the forlorn Adam
Keeps wandering in misery!

Memories rain in my mind
Of the greatest Friend of sinners,
Who found me by the wayside;
Judged and condemned by the mob.

They were all 'saints',
'Spotless and sinless';
And they feigned
As if they were agents of God!

They believed that they owned God;
That the Creator was their 'property'
Until the Creator, in human form,
Turned up, clad in the dust of the street!

I was an outcast, and I knew that;
I lived on the fringes and no one cared for me.
No one asked me what I ate
And no one asked me if I had a gown to wear!
But, when I sinned for bread,
Everyone knew!

Son of God, the Reader of hearts,
Read my heart and my life.
He alone saw the angst of my soul
Yearning for love, which was misplaced!

He sat on the ground,
On the soil wet with the day before's rain,
To be one with soiled creatures like me;
The Judge and culprit on the same ground!

He started writing the stories of mankind,
Stories of every man and every woman
From the beginning of time,
On the soil that was wet.

Man was created from soil, He wrote.
And scribbled the tales of the soiled men.
"From the soil that is wet with raining tears
Are re-created new men and new women!"

There was dust everywhere,
In the whole atmosphere;
Waiting for a rain to fall
And wet the soil for a creation new!

Everyone had a stone in his hand
And you know, a stone is hardened soil!
Hardened like hearts of stone!

'Throw the first stone,
You who have never sinned!"
And everyone dropped his stone
One by one, and left the place.

I was feeling a rain within,
Pouring down in full,
Wetting my soiled soul
And molding me into a new shape!

And He wrote in my soul,
With the finger of the Creator
A new tale of love and redemption
For ages to ponder and be cleansed!

He became my song and my sunshine
And I lived in the light of His grace.
My soil became an island
Full of blossoms of everlasting love!

Until the hour my Sun was set
In the middle of this unhappy day.
When my Master died on the Cross
After the most agonizing torments.

Do you know how it feels
Sitting lonely in the rain?
To bereave the Beloved,
- God and Master?

Do you know
How it feels to lose God?
To lose the perennial rain
Pouring down on the soil of our souls?
And the gracious fingers
That scribble tales of love
On our wet souls?

Do you know why the world is a wilderness,
With dried up hearts and silenced songs?
It has lost its God and Master;
It has lost its rain of grace!

Nay,
I will sing the song of rain

The whole night until the dawn
Of the Third day,
When the Sun shall rise again
From the heart of the rain.

And the new light of the risen Sun
Will create new radiant souls
Out of our soiled tales,
For the world to read and be radiant!

****

THE TEARS OF A ROCK

Once you called me 'The Rock';
Now, every rock on earth mocks me!
I, the impulsive, the daring Peter,
Who once bragged to die for his Master!

Beside this fireplace that burns bright,
I shiver with a chill as deep as my being!
It is so cold here!
I am lost in an icy sea
Like a lone seaman who has lost his oars.
A shipwreck
Of trust and faith…!

Where have I lost the hand of grace
That once held me
When I started drowning
In the middle of the raging sea?

"Woman, I do not know Him!"
The words of my denial
Is still resounding in my soul;
I know not who I am;
I have become a stranger to me.
I, whom the Lord called 'The Rock'!

And He looks
From the shadow of this mournful night
Like a diamond that shines in the darkness.
His look tears my heart apart,
Which I once bragged 'as solid as the Rock!'

Oh No!
I can't face the rays from His eyes,
I shrink like a man
Who had spent ages in a dark dungeon!

It is like the primordial 'Light'
That shone in the void
At the utterance of the divine Word:
"Let there be Light!"

Memories flood in my heart
Like the waters of Jordan
Drops of cleansing fall upon my soul
Like the Baptist's anointing.

And in the river, I see myself
My roots, my origin…
A frivolous fisherman,
Who wandered in the Sea of Galilee
And its sprawling banks;
Fretting and fuming
At everyone around.

One day, a slim and tall Galilean
With a sparkling pair of eyes,
Cast a net into our hearts and said:
"I shall make you fishers of men!"

Not knowing what he really meant,
I set out, charmed by his fiery eyes.

I have seen miracles galore,
I have heard mysteries laid bare,
I have spent a night on Tabor
With the greats like Moses and Elijah!

I have seen seas becalmed,
And storms turning meek
At His fiery words.
He, the tamer of nature
And wild human souls.

I have seen Him wash the feet
Of frivolous fishermen!
Awestruck by his humility,
I almost averted him.
But with love that has no equal,
He went on and washed us all.

I have seen him break the bread
In a sacrificial fashion,
Whose inestimable depths
I have yet to fathom!

He has said about the cross
And his inglorious death on it,
Which I could never digest.
How can the tamer of nature
And the Master of all creation
Die like a culprit on a cross?
I can't think of him dying;
I love him so much!
And I would lay down my own life
To spare him from death.
Yes, it's true
That I have said those words.

But, on this chilly night,
All my spirits have failed,
And I feel so cold and scared;
Nay,
This is what I am,
A coward inside,
With a deep desire to love
But with no courage to prove it!

O Lord, I see everything
In the Jordan of my soul,
Every detail of my life,
Every little spark of your love
That lifted me up from a muddy seashore.

And I crumble!
I crumble like a rock
Torn apart from within.
How can the shell resist
Once the core has melted down?
I am broken from the core!

Through the breakage of the core,
The rays of your eyes seep in!
And I begin to see!
The Jordan, springing from my soul,
Now oozes down through my eyes!
No, it is not just tears,
It is the waters of redemption,
In which I flow back to my Master!

And He is there,
Beyond time and space,
Ever wounded with those thorns on head,
Waiting for me with outstretched hands,
Like the Father of that parable;
And I am back in his bosom,
Not just a rock,
But a diamond with his light within!

****

THE FIERY TOUCH

(A poetic look at the healing of the woman with hemorrhage)

A drop of blood fell
And disappeared in the sea -
The frosty, dark sea of men and women
Thronging, and jamming each other
On the bustling streets of Galilee.

For the Galilean was passing by,
Casting smiles and cures
On everyone around
With a compassion unseen hitherto!

Drops of blood fell again.
And the sea of men began to blush
With rage and horror;
And a ripple of outrage
Swept through the sea of men!

The Son of Man's voyages,
Ever since He was born
Into that cold, frosty night,
Was thus:
Through cold streets of frozen men,
Where hardly any lamp
Of faith or love burned!

This crowd was no different;
Men and women of cold hearts.
And Jesus sailed through the chilly sea of men!

It was then the woman set sail her boat
Into the cold, frosty sea of men!
She had a blazing torch in her heart;
A torch burning with faith unmatched
And a desire as fierce as fire.

Her 'leaking' little boat slithered over the sea,
Squeezing forward through the tumultuous mob…
Yonder stood the Son of Man, encased
In the shell of guarding minions
Who fancied that God was theirs alone!

For years, she had been living
In the peripheries, like an outcast.
A woman with downcast eyes and life,
She hid herself from the public.
But now, a mystic fire from within
Whispered to her soul:
"The day of your redemption has come!"

That was how she lighted her torch of faith
And set sail on her little 'leaking' boat
To traverse the dark, frosty sea of men.

Torn between desire and shame,
She stood before the fortress of the minions.
Her right index finger became a wick,
Which caught fire from her soul's torch.

She saw the fringe of the Lord's cloak
Hanging down onto the ripples of the human sea.
With a gush of desire and faith,
She touched the fringe with her fiery finger.

And the Lord's attire caught fire!

The fire climbed upwards
Burning all the way up…
His skin, his flesh and finally
His holy heart!

His heart melted like wax in the heat:
And the balm of healing
Oozed out of it into her,
Healing her wholly!

The Lord felt a sensation of heat
In the midst of that cold sea,
And was surprised to the core!

Who, in that frosty sea,
Has come with a fiery touch?
And He turned and quizzed:
"Who touched me?"

****

SANDALS FROM ETERNITY

To step down from eternity,
He needed a pair of sandals;
Simple ones, made of leather.

Just as He wore the garb of flesh
To be one with the humans,
He needed a pair of leather sandals
To be in touch with the fauna.

The sandals were carefully chosen,
To tread all the distance
From eternity to the alleyway of time,
And stroll through the pathways of time!

The dusty streets of Galilee knew
The soft, delicate touch of those sandals;
And they were ecstatic
When the sandals of the Master Wayfarer
Moved over them.

Over hills and valleys,
Over the seashores of Galilee,
On the pathways of Judea,
Capernaum and Bethany…
The sandals marched on;
The eternity was moving on
The pathways of time!

Divinity was walking
Down the history lane,
Starting from the Garden of Eden.
From Ur to the land of Canaan,
To Egypt; and back again to the Promised Land
Through the sea that was split
And through the parched wilderness.
Through the heat of the fiery pillar
And cool shadow of the pillar of cloud.

The sandaled walk of God!

It bore all the dust
From Ur, Canaan, Egypt, Red Sea
And the wilderness;
As the mark of an ever-abiding love!

And it would bear all the dust
Of fallen human race;
From Adam's sin to the end of time!

At the Jordan,
As he heard the footsteps coming near
Through the sprawling vales of history,
The Big Baptist was all ears.

John then had a vision:
All the heaven and the angels
Kneeling in homage
On a pair of sandals

That strolled on the streets of Galilee!
The whole universe,
With its galaxies and cosmic voids,
Shrunk into that little lampstand
Of Eternal Light!

Awestruck and overwhelmed,
The man, clad in camel's hair, exclaimed:
"I am not worthy to untie
The straps of His sandals!"

****

IN THE WELL OF DREAMS

A rainbow vanished from the sky above,
Seen through the gaping mouth of the well.
Joseph writhed in pain and despair,
Gazing at his dreams waning yonder.

Colorless sky, with a silenced song,
Looked like the grave of a shattered dream.
The stars on the twilight sky
Seemed like the shreds of a motley coat.

In this well, the graveyard of my dreams,
I stand lonely and broken.
Knots of brotherhood are in shreds
And I have lost the colors of love!

Desolation encircles me
Like this waterless well;
I feel cut off from humanity
And the Fatherhood of divinity.

Darkness of the soul,
The endless expanse of the wilderness,
That every seeker of God
Has to tread on his way to liberation.

Who has planted the seeds of dreams
In poor and frail human souls?
And who takes them away half-grown,
Before the dawn of fulfillment?

What is wrong in chasing dreams?
Can life progress without dreams?
What is wrong in sharing dreams,
And revel in my own dreams?

I was the center and monarch
In all my dreams hitherto;
I loved praises and accolades
And wished to sail on ego.

I loved multi-colored garments
And the sheen of limelight.
I loved pampers and cuddles
And shunned every bitter cure.

Now that I am stripped of my motley coat,
I stand naked before Your eyes, Lord!
Colorless as my bare soul
Just as you see me from my birth.

I shed my frills and flounces
To face You as I am, as I am…
This well is my Garden of Eden
And I begin anew right here.

In this well, in this wilderness,
I exchange my dreams and all their colors
With the singular dream of the Creator,
Which He dreamed in timeless eternity!

Whoa! I see the rainbow back again
Ascending on my colorless sky
And a motley of radiant hues
Drape my soul with graces new!

New blossoms of humanity
Bloom in the graveyards of gloom.
A new brotherhood dawns
And a new kingdom rises.

Beyond the desert, beyond the Nile
A new strain of song rises
That sings of a timeless dream
Brimming with bliss and peace!

****

FATHER

(This poem explores the thoughts of Saint Francis of Assisi, when he was disowned by his biological father Pietro di Bernardone, who also demanded his son to give back everything he had received from him, including the attires he wore. Standing naked in body and soul, Francis then implores the Heavenly Father to clothe him. This poem also has ecological undertones.)

Clad me with your love, my Father!

For I am naked, rejected and disowned!

I stand here;

Between heaven and earth,

With no cloud to conceal my nakedness,

Nor a leaf to hide my shame!

I am no one's son;

And my soul falls into the abyss of agony;

The agony of every orphan

From the beginning of time!

I hear a cry

Rising from the valley of the unloved,

The wailing of the fatherless,

The song of the orphans!

Shelter me, my Father,

Oh Father!

Clad me with your sky,

Drape me with your love.

I am a baby, reborn

Out of this abandonment,

This rejection and this orphanhood!

I curl back into the womb of my mother,

The earth.
Recoil to form an offspring again.
Beget me, my Father!
Once again-
To take a new life!
Let your greenest daughter, the earth
Hide me in her womb,
Nurture me with her juices,
Make me one with her offsprings,
My siblings,
So that I may emerge once again
Your child,
And the brother of all your creation!
Come on green grass, my sister,
Lull me the divine lullabies
And teach me the praise of nature!
Come on thin breeze, my brother,
Sing me the melodies of the spirit,
And fill me with the breath of the Creator!
Come on' you mother earth,
Teach me the secret of the green
And the harmony of nature!
Yeah, Father!
I am sailing back to my roots,
To the Garden of Eden,
Luxuriant with divine greeneries…
I recoil into the soil,
Melt into the mud,
And breathe out my spirit…
I can feel your nostrils my Father!

The breath of love ineffable
Flowing from your heart!
Where the Son was begotten,
And from where the Spirit emanated!
Wow! The tremendous Fatherhood!
And I feel the terrific 'son-hood'!
The mighty breath rising
And flowing through
The divine windpipe,
Loving and begetting 'me'!
The green is mine,
The earth is mine,
The river is mine and so is the sky!

'Don't play in the soil!"
Rises my father's voice
From my previous life;
I can recall it as if in a dream.
"Don't touch the mud! It's dirty!"
He shouts with a kick on my head!
And I felt the earth moist with tears,
All sweat, with wet mud!
My Father, Peter Bernardone,
Pulls me back with force!
And I am alone,
Encaged, encased and encroached!
I heard the rivulet sobbing,
And the breeze returning
After an unanswered knock
At my door!
With an arrogant cloak

I shunned the breeze,
And with a pair of regal sandals
I built a fence
Against the soil and the earth!
I became a kingdom
With my own autonomy!
The sky became a stranger,
Something so aloof,
Whom I never gave a gaze to!
The rain wept and shed her tears
On my roof;
And I turned away my eyes
From the pool of her sorrow
Spread on my courtyard!
That was how I lost my mother, the earth,
And her green secret!

And it required the rejection of my father
For me to finally realize
The loss of my mother
The green earth!

Now beget me my Father in heaven!
Beget me once again!

Yeah! I can feel my mother!
I can feel her bosom,
Luxuriant with the greenery,
The grass, the herbs and the trees;
And her moist tenderness
With rivers and streams flowing!

Hi Sun, my brother,
Hi Moon, my sister,
Hi Breeze, my little brother,
Tell me about your Creator,
The Father, who created you and me!

Time stands still!
Night and day have united,
The Sun and the Moon
Sing hand in hand.
Days and nights
Belong to the mortals!
To those who have been cut off
From nature, our mother!
Brotherhood is beyond time
And beyond space;
It happens in the heart of God,
The Father and the Creator,
Who has no beginning or end!

****

Who says I am naked now?
Can't you see?
Love is my cloak
And brotherhood my mantle.
The nature, the pristine of creations,
With nothing vile in the eyes,
Sees nothing weird in me,
In my nakedness,
My primordial purity,
My very 'pure' self,
Just as my 'Father' sees me!"

Here,
In this midnight pasture,
Beneath the starry sky,
On this lonely rock,
How free am I?
With a pair of wings within
I fly up and down
Between heaven and earth;
The mountains and the seas,
The heights and the depths!
I gaze up to the majestic sky
With stars sprinkled all over!

My Father,
Lower the blanket, star-studded.
Let me feel you,
Hiding behind!
Pearls of eternal light
Shall sparkle,
And wipe off
The darkness in my 'self'.
The celestial crystals
Shall roll within,
Chiming like divine bells!

The sky that Adam beheld
Upon his primordial loneliness;
Comforting and caressing from above…
The firmament Abraham saw,
Studded with stars

That none on earth could count!
The sky of Israel
With a ladder hung down
For the angels to move up and down…

Speak from the sky,
My Father!
Yes, my Abba,
I can see the heap of stones!
I can see a broken heart
In the shape of a fallen church;
Isolated stones
With a broken brotherhood!
This stone says:
"I am the church!"
And that stone retorts:
"No, I am the church, you are not!"
A third one growls:
"None of you,
It's me alone!"

Father,
Now I know
Why they have lost
The single sky!
Each one has
Their own 'God'
Inflated with 'Ego';
And one can't see
The 'God' in the other!

How can there be a church
In a heap of warring stones!

And now
You ask me Father,
To beg for stones!

Hey,
I can hear
The thundering voice
Of your Son, the Redeemer:
"Remove the stone!"
Yes, remove the stone!
Let the life come out.
Set him free,
From the cave of decay!

Hey,
Give me a stone, brother!
Giggling?
Throwing? At me?
Take it easy, brother,
I forgive you!
But, please remove the stone
From your heart!
It is too heavy for you –
That Ego!
The church needs stones
Taken out of hearts.
Nay,

The church needs hearts
With stones taken out!

****

Oh!
The darkness of the loneliness
Encircles me;
An endless wilderness
Is all I can see.
I look on,
I look on and on…
Out of the wilderness
She rises,
The golden-haired Claire!
The enchantress of my younger days…
She appears and reappears
In my dreams;
My old harp mourns within
And breaks out into angst, profound.
That is when
The amorous birds perch
On the branch upon my head
And begin a mate dance…
Adam should have Eve!
Even you, my Father
Willingly joined their hearts!
I am single! So single!
Oh! This wilderness is unending…
Thirst within is growing…
A drop…?

Yes, a drop now falls,
And rolls down my cheek,
I am a human, my Father,
Adam's Son
With all his passions inherited!
The Eve hides among the clouds,
And vanishes in the sky!
Oh! Heavens, take my masculinity!
Oh! Wind of brotherhood,
Come, and blow off these rain clouds,
Pregnant with a flood of romance!

Father,
Take me to your bosom,
In the warmth of your fatherhood,
Where I become a baby again
With my passions unborn;
Where masculinity and femininity
Merge into humanity…
Here, I shed one more attire,
The attire of my wild passions,
And I become naked again,
The nakedness of soul,
With no gender mark on it!
Come Claire, come!
Let me touch your soul
With the feather of my soul.
Feel with me
The flight of the spirit
And soar with me

To the thin air of the angels.

****

Oh Gubbio,
You say you are scared.
I can see an abyss in your collective eyes.
Where hope has drowned,
Faith has drowned…
I know, Gubbio
The reason for your fear.

The tale is a long one…
A journey from 'we'
To 'you' and 'me',
Then to 'it' and 'me'!
That was when the 'green'
Began to vanish from your soul,
Little by little,
Part by part…
Think of it,
When did it begin?
Tell me,
 When did you lose
Your Father -
Your everyone's Father!
You withdrew,
Then you shrank
From her, the green sister.
You became 'I'
And she became 'it'!

And the Father became
'My Father'
And no more 'Our Father!'

Take heart, Gubbio!
This is a simple surgery.
It is just a matter of
Replacing an eye,
An eye with its roots in your heart.
An eye that sees
The soul within,
Not the outer cover
That frightens you
Or abhors you!

See!
See how the wolf transforms!
How the red, bloodshot eyes
Reflect the splendor of a sunset!
How the wounds of a soul
Is manifested!
The ancient, unhealed wounds!
See!
It is bleeding for acceptance,
Bleeding for love!
Look!
See through the white teeth,
See the lilies hiding within
Sail back to his past,
The tiny wolf,

Sucking his mother,
With a string of lilies
Just peeping out
From his tiny mouth!
See him there,
Right there, Gubbio.
Discover his tenderness
Beneath his mother's arms.
And learn that
Every wild transformation
Has an angelic beginning!
Find out the moment of wound,
And repair the moment.

Let's walk ahead!
Come, with me Gubbio,
Take that stone out of your heart
Bring out your naked soul!
Here is the rendezvous
Of souls, of souls!

Hi, my brother Wolf!
Your brother salutes you!
We have one Father,
One common Father
Who loves you and me.
Come with me to the garden
The Garden of brotherhood
Where there is no man or wolf,
But children of God, the Father!

Let us meet there,
Beneath the canopy
Of divine Fatherhood.
Don't weep, my brother,
I can sense your agony.
I sense your loneliness,
The first moment
Of your isolation!
The moment
You gave in to the wild passion.
It was your way of reaction
To the stolen brotherhood,
Rejected love!
Bring that paw,
Put it here, brother.
Here, in my palms!
Yes,
That way! Exactly!
Now who will tell us
That we are not brothers?
Tell them that
We have the same Father!

Listen Gubbio!
Remember this lesson
For the rest of your life.
There is nothing wilder
Outside you
Than the wildest passion -
The whirlwind of your Ego!

Tame that wolf,
And every wolf will turn
Your friend and brother!

****

34

GOD'S CRYSTAL CASEMENT

A soft light drizzled
Upon the misty glass pane of that Jewish window.
The Jewish girl in her teens
Gazed at those misty sketches,
Now brightened,
With wide-open eyes!

On the mist that had started melting softly,
She demystified and recalled
The history of her people -
Their long wait for the Messiah,
With a delicate feminine sigh.

She decoded the map of Israel's journeys
Down from the days of Adam,
From the meandering lines on the mist…
On every lip was His name,
In every heart was His air…
When will He come – the Messiah?

The humblest of the girls of that hamlet,
She lived a life as light as a song.
On the wing of a song,
Her soul often flew so high,
Higher than any mortal could fly.

In her blue eyes bloomed,
All the lilies of Carmel.
On her rosy lips resounded,
All the praises of heaven.
Yet, she loved the lowliest paths,
And curled in the cocoon of silence.

The light on the window
Sparkled on the mist
With an ethereal glow!
And a beauteous smile
Bloomed on the mist.
Around the smile,
A figure took shape;
A human countenance
More handsome than any!

The whole mist then melted down
And the Messenger of heaven shone bright!
Opening the tiny window of time,
The voice of eternity resounded:
"Hail O favored one!
The Lord is with you!"

Startled stood the young girl,
Who had never feigned holiness;
Always the handmaid of the Lord,
Mary sought only the feet of the Lord!

Favored one? I?
Of all the women of nobility
In all the cities and towns in the world,
How come the angel comes to me?
Who am I but a humble Jewish girl?

The voice of the Godhead
Echoed through the angel's mouth
Like a music unheard hitherto
By any mortal in history!

The girl is chosen with an eternal decree
To be the Mother of God, the Son!
And He would descend on this planet
Through this blessed gateway!

She would be the crystal casement
Through which men would look up to God;
And the perfect mirror
That reflects the radiance of divinity!

Opening the window of her soul,
The maiden welcomed the Word
With these humble words:
"Behold the handmaid of the Lord,
Be it done to me as per your Word!"

The tiny room was lit up at once
By the splendor of 'Logos'.
The Word resounded

Like the music of heaven;
And the cool morning air
Became a seraphic symphony!

38

****

THE END